Perfect Capitalism Manifesto

You're Welcome

DENVER, COLORADO

To Begin:

FACT

The current form of capitalism will collapse
(Still the biggest fan of capitalism,
Just not in its current form is all)

Few short things before we get started just to quickly gives some reasons why and then we shall begin.

1. Cost of living keeps going up (Already to expensive, personal experience: Single, no kids, I make 15 and hour, have half my health insurance covered, company car, and still have trouble getting by.)

2. Look at the housing market, and think, if I seek a profit on my house, and each owner thereafter:

   Are cheapest houses will eventually be well into the hundreds of thousands and so on.

There is going to be no chapters... Just ganna be winging it, been holding these ideas up in the noggin for quite some time. They would all blend together anyways.

So where should would start this fixing economics journey?

I shall start it with a big what if...

What if I teamed up with all the richest people in the world and they gave me all their money, and they said... We want you to take this money (Trillions? Right? Probably more?) and fix everything.

This is what I would do...

First things first. Higher the best mathematicians and business people in the world.

Cost of living:

What we need to do is get the cost of living down to make your money worth more. So what im going to suggest is going to upset you for a minute or two, but stick with me. Anybody that works in the basic needs (Food, water, electric, gas, man-ufacturing) should take a cut in pay and have a salary cap. Let me do a little math and you will see what im talking about.

I make 15 bucks and hour/ 40 hours a week = 600 bucks a week = 2400 a month

I pay 500 rent (cheap anymore) + 200 heat and electric + 100 a week for food (400) + 25 water = 1125 a month

so... 2400-1125 = 1275 a month for other (expensive) items

Now lets say we take a cut in pay and fix housing

7 bucks and hour/ 40 hours a week = 280 bucks a week = 1120

I pay 75 rent + 30 heat and electric + 15 bucks a week for food + 5 water = 125

so 1120-125 = 995 a month for other (cheap) items

So if your not in basic needs.... and you make 15 bucks an hour then...

2400-125 = 2275 extra

You just made everyones money worth more, you make almost the exact same, not to mention all the products our cheaper so it will go a lot further.

So our main goal is to make our basic needs as cheap as possible, even if it meant the company (get into this in a bit) paid for part of it.

People that work in these basic needs would be modern day economic heroes.

Housing:

So we have to fix housing, no other way around it, we can't have our houses getting more and more expensive.

So I say we use this system...

1 bedroom and 1 bath = x amount of dollars

2 bedroom and 2 bath = x amount of dollars

and so on and so on...

No matter how nice the house it

And to figure out how to price it we find the cheapest contractors and ask them how much to make a decent...

1 bedroom and 1 bath

2 bedroom.... etc

and thats what the cap is.

Now no one is saying you can't do whatever to your house and make it as nice as you want, but when you sell it, you can only sell it for as much as the cap is...

Couple things are going to happen, probably more houses will stay in a family, be a lot easier to move, and with all that extra money that people will have they will actually be nice homes for really good prices. Imagine mortgage payments of a $100 or most likely less on a beautiful home.

Rent same thing.. There will be caps.

Now some of you are thinking but I already paid so much for this house and can't take the hit. Thats what I will be using some of the money for. Id be paying off the difference between the new price of the house and what you paid whether you already paid it off or not. So take it and pay off your house or get it re mortgaged, or if its extra, save it for retirement, or buy something nice, or you can let me keep it as a donation... Whatever

And also, maybe for houses directly on lakes or beaches we could use the normal housing method, so we would still see some turnaround on those. Otherwise no one is ever going to sell there 20,000 house on the beach... know what im saying?

But with the offset market I would still be giving some money to people with beach houses and lake houses because the price would come down a bit and i want to make it fair for everybody.

No one gets the raw end of the deal

Health care:

Quick one and will get back more on it later.

One of the reasons health care is so high is because of how high college is, especially med school. College prices will already go way down with the cost of living costs. But also instead of having to pay such massive salaries to new med students due to such high loan debt we do this.

We pay their college expenses so they are debt free when they go into the med field in exchange they agree to a price cap for lets say 10 years (training years, for the most part, anyways). A fair price cap, and they get the enjoyment of doing what they love and not having any school loans to worry about. We will actually make money on this not to mention will drop our insurance costs way down.

The business:

Stick with me...

Liberals, you are about to hate me for a minute or two, but by the end of this you will love it.

Now what to do will all that money... Im going to privatize everything, separate the private sector and gov't completely, and probably add another gov't within the private sector.

And here is how I'm going to that...

I'm going to start buying every single last company, and with that money I make from all those im going to buy more until I own every single company in the world. Not to own them, but to make every company owner debt free. Then I would give them their company back take, take 20% of their profit, and have them work for not salary, but for 80% of the profit.

They would have no income tax whatsoever, along with everyone else.

Now im not going to have anything to do with running that company, and its still capitalism like always. No picking winners or losers, the competition is still on.

So I own but not run everything, what about new companies?

I always had an idea where if I had a lot of money and a big company that I would put idea boxes all over the place and hire some of the best business men to sort through my employees ideas. And If they had a good Idea I would invest in it for them, so they would be debt free, they could either take a lump sum, or they could run it themselves, or any possible scenario, we would work out a deal. It could be as little as a t-shirt idea, we set a price, we decide percentages and we sell it. Then maybe you don't make a million, but even if you made an extra 1000 bucks on the side it would be cool.

So thats how the entire company would run, Im not running any of the companies, you are, but you have a practically endless amount of money ready to invest in one of your ideas, debt free, no worries for you.

Now go back to everyone making extra money, no taxes on anything because im already taking 20% on companies, everything is cheap. And you will all have extra money for the finer things in life, go out to restaurants, movies, video games, vacations, super bowl parties, presents, baseball games, etc, etc.

There will be so many jobs it won't even be funny. It may actually become a problem of having to many jobs and not enough employees.

There would be such a thing as making to much money, you have a company that starts making many millions or billions a year or whatever. You would be given the great honor of having to be put on salary and also get a plaque and a nice watch, and a ceremony. Now this salary would still be millions a year. And depending on the company, it would most likely be guaranteed for life. Like say you had a company that made a billion dollars and provided all those jobs and it ends up going out of business. You would still remain on salary because it had already made way more than that. See what im saying? Keeping it fair and keeping the American dream alive.

Now as your employer, I would like to offer you all health insurance... That simple

Now my company is going to have a ton of extra money, and everyone will have jobs except for people with bad disabilities or mental conditions. But of course, as good human beings, we will take care of them.

We will also take care of the roads, and any of those sorta things.

Food stamps, medicaid, yadda yadda, will all be things of the past.

Plus we will continue with research and development. We only have so much oil, so we have to continue to try to figure out something to save future generations the trouble. Have to figure out how to make more oil, or get that cold fusion going. Something alternative.

Retirement, We would have to figure out the age, I would like to see it somewhere in the 50-55 range if we could (That is why i hired the mathematicians and businessmen for). Now everyone would get the same social security, whether you retired a pizza delivery man or CEO of a huge company) Probably be minimum wage 40 hour a week. And if you want more than that in your later years, save accordingly, but you will still live good either way.

Labor army:

Now were going to be having so many jobs available that a lot of people would not want to do those hard jobs for low costs of pay (but still good, and make a great living, and very personally rewarding) in those basic necessity jobs. And I also know there are a lot of different ideas for how we should handle manual labor jobs. After taking into consideration, I believe I have the fairest way to do it possible.

So labor army, which would be a manual labor union so to speak. You would sign up in high school (or possibly later) and just like the regular army it would be for 4 years. First, we would send you to college, where you can major in anything you want, chase whatever dream you have but as a minor or around 3 credits a semester would be training for what job or jobs you will have in the Labor army. Now if you want to join and your not really interested in a chance to get a bachelors, we would still want you to go to college and take the minimum 3 credits a semester and still get that college experience, meeting friends, good learning environment, networking, stories for a lifetime, all that jazz. But we would like to you to see it as a chance to make yourself a renaissance man or woman. By majoring in something or picking up different minors. Which i think we should start offering other crafts such as electrician, plumbing, machining, to college curriculums. Use that time for whatever you want.

So you signed up for the 4 year labor army. Hows it going to go? Well your first 6 months to a year your going to be doing the jobs nobody wants to do and then it just gets easier from there. We all take a turn at the real "bad" jobs, and we try to make it as fast a cycle as possible.

What we have to do is level every job, go through the entire world and mark the manual jobs from hard to easiest and put them in levels. So the more years you put in the easier or more enjoyable the jobs you can apply for become. And as we make a new business with manual labor jobs we level it. And as well with just getting easier, more lucrative positions open up as you can move out of the basic necessities category. So say you went into the labor army and started out making 7 an hour on a pipeline, you might retire delivering pizza's for 15-20 bucks an hour or something to that extent. You see where im going with it.

So those first 4 years we would put you where we need to,

and you could sign up if you wanted to stay domestic or travel the world or whatever.

After 4 years your in, then when you sign up for another year, apply anywhere that you are at a high enough level for.

Now if your going to be moving out of the manual labor into the non labor workforce, we would just want clear notice and enough time to fill your position. We got to get work done, but we also don't want you to miss out on your dream job either.

And when you leave your level just stays the same, and if you ever come back, you just start at the level you left at. So you may be a CEO of a company someday with a level 5 labor card or whatever. Something to fall back on.

And remember, those idea boxes are always there, so you can always make some extra money or with the right idea be running your own company or retired that day.

Drugs:

I am all about freedom and people doing whatever they want as long as they are not impeaching on other peoples freedoms. To quote Ben Harper "If your causing no harm your alright with me".

I would get rid of crack, heroine, meth, bath salts, and possibly acid. Not because you should not have the freedom to do it. But because look at the facts, What % of those people on those drugs commit crimes? which violates other peoples freedoms.

Now a trained specialized army should be in charge of distribution, Because if we just sell everything over the counter our young children are going to get there hands on them. These dealers would sell to whoever, but only so much at a time, and develop relationships, and be trained to not sell it to people who just turn around and sell it for a profit to kids that should not be getting them. And dealers would have selections like any other kind of store with great selections and all different kinds of brands and so forth.

Now I would still make it illegal to then start your own selling operation or anything like that. We would want it all done by trained professionals.

Now some people can smoke weed and do anything, drive whatever. But it would not be a crime to do, but we would suggest if you ever did feel your ability was impaired to just pull over and wait the half hour or whatever until the high goes away. If a cop pulled up to your parked car an asked what was wrong, got to high and needed to stop driving would be a valid excuse.

Gambling:

Would be legal, and remember because how much they make, the owners would most likely be on salary and profits going to the company. So if you make money great, and if you don't, well at least you know where it went. Back into investing and health care and all that good stuff.

Take care of women amendment:

Now the company is going to be raking in the money so we should have enough money to do this. But I just don't feel woman were meant to work, if they want to, all the more power to them, and anything is open to them. But they are the light of the world, not to mention bring life to the world and should be treated as such. So to any single female out of mom and dads house. You would have the option not to work, we will pay your cost of living and give you a little spending money while you wait for mister right. Just as soon as you get a job, or move in with a man, or get married you would be taken off the payroll. I think I speak for all men, especially those with daughters that they should be taken care of no matter what. By all means even if you decide not to work, get your diploma, go to college, get educated still.

Abortion:

My personal stance. The fetus begins to grow its brain at week 4, which is when I would consider it a life. So anything after week 4 your keeping it. So if you don't want a kid, Birth control and maybe add in a pregnancy test every 2 to 3 weeks to be sure.

I think that about sums it up for now. Should be enough to get everything started.

I will leave you with two questions

1. What if there were no what if's?

2. WWJD? <== I think he would agree with me on this one.

www.ingramcontent.com/pod-product-compliance
Lightning Source LLC
Chambersburg PA
CBHW030106300526
45785CB00019B/2778